WHEN HAVING IT ALL STILL HURTS

FROM PRO ATHLETE TO MOTHER AND WIFE — A
MEMOIR ABOUT THE ACHE NO ONE SEES COMING

RASHANDA MCCANTS JOHNSON

This is for every woman who has ever felt invisible, even in a crowded room.

To the mothers who break generational curses with whispered prayers and tired hands.

To the wives who smile through silence.

To the daughters who carry more than they were ever meant to hold.

This book is for the ones who seem strong—because they had no other choice.

To my mother, Brenda *— you survived what should've killed you more than once. You are proof. I am the echo.*
Pieces of you have stitched together everything I am.

To my husband, Chris *— your steady strength gave me space to come undone.*
You saw me—when I didn't even recognize myself.

To Reya—my rainbow, my mirror, my "why."
I did every hard thing, told every truth, to leave you a world where softness isn't earned through suffering. May you grow free.

To the girl who lived *— you made it. Now tell the truth.*
Even when it hurts.

PREFACE

I didn't sit down to write this book because I had the time. I wrote it because the silence finally felt louder than the truth.

It began with a mammogram I had avoided for over a year—not because I forgot, but because I was afraid. Afraid of the pain, yes. But more than that, afraid of what I already knew deep down: that my body might be carrying a silent threat. The same one that visited my mother. My aunt. My grandmother.

Breast cancer was an uninvited inheritance passed down like a whisper. And at 38, even with a negative BRCA gene result, I knew better than to feel safe.

I finally made the appointment. I showed up. In the hushed chill of that sterile room, I pressed my body against cold machinery and found something unexpected: connection. The woman taking my images was a mother too. A keeper of secrets. A woman who knew the weight of smiling through a hollow ache. We talked. Not just in passing pleasantries—but soul to soul. About how easy it is to look full on the outside and feel invisible within.

She saw me.

In that mirror, I finally saw myself too.

Then came the callback.

Dense breast tissue. Higher risk. More imaging. More waiting.

I shut down. I stopped eating. I told no one. It wasn't the healthiest response, but it was honest. For days, I lived between two sentences:

"We'll see you next year," or "We need to talk about chemo."

That in-between space cracked something open. The weight I'd carried for years—through motherhood, marriage, grief, pressure, and perfection—was no longer content to stay contained. It demanded air. And this book became my way of breathing again.

When Having It All Still Hurts is not a story about blame or bitterness.

It's not a how-to.

It's a how-I-survived.

It's a mirror for the woman who shows up tired and still gives her best.

For the mother who wonders if presence is enough.

For the wife who loves deeply but sometimes forgets how to love herself.

This book is for every woman who's ever whispered, "I'm fine," while silently unraveling.

It's for the daughters who became caretakers.

For the breadwinners turned homemakers.

For the ones who hold the world together—even while they're falling apart.

This is my truth.

Offered with open hands and a trembling but courageous heart.

If you find yourself in these pages, know that you are not alone. Even when it hurts. Especially when it hurts. You are still worthy of joy, healing, and peace. This is my story.

I wrote it for you.

— **Rashanda McCants Johnson**

CONTENTS

INTRODUCTION

I was supposed to feel grateful.

I had a husband. The house. The beautiful baby girl. A past that some would kill for—a jersey, a legacy, a name that still echoes in gyms I haven't stepped foot in for years. I had survived more than most. Loved deeper than most. Accomplished what I set out to do. And still...

Something inside me was quietly unraveling.

Not all at once—and never in public. Not in ways that would alarm anyone. But in the quiet spaces between preschool drop-offs and dinner plates, between brushed teeth and real estate closings, between stretch marks and stitched wounds, something ached. Not the ache that makes you scream—the kind that makes you silent.

It's strange when your dreams come true — and you can't find yourself inside them.

For years, I wore my strength like armor. I knew how to win. I knew how to lead. I knew how to survive. No one teaches you how to live when survival is no longer the assignment. When the very things you once prayed for become the weight you can't put down.

This book is about that space. The space between having it all and still hurting, anyway.

It's about womanhood in its rawest form. The kind no one claps for. It's about legacy—the one I inherited, the one I've carried, and the one I'm still creating for my daughter. It's about marriage, not as a fairytale, but as a mirror. About motherhood as both gift and ghost. It's about trauma that lingers and healing that doesn't always arrive with clarity or closure.

More than anything, this is a book about being truly seen. Even when your smile says, "I'm fine" and your spirit whispers, "I'm not."

If you have ever been so overwhelmed in your kitchen that you cried into the sink...

If you have ever felt the crushing weight of family responsibilities while losing yourself...

If you have ever wondered why joy feels like pressure...

If you have ever considered quitting but continued, ...

This is for you.

GIRL IN THE BACKGROUND

I was the middle child of three—the quiet one, the observer who mastered the art of disappearing. The one who watched everything and said very little. I guarded secrets—my own and those of others—revealing them only exacerbated problems. Even as a kid, I knew silence was safer.

Contradictions formed the foundation of my childhood. My father did not believe in God. My mother did. Not with scripture-covered walls or Sunday school memory verses—but she believed. She believed in her own way, just enough to whisper "thank you, Lord" when things got heavy. But when she said it, my father would bark back, "Thank who? Get somewhere with that propaganda bullshit!" The room would go still. My loyalty stretched thin between the two people who gave me life. Whose side do you choose when both parents are right and wrong in different ways?

My father, James, resembled a warning. Tall, lean, with a sharpness in his jaw and eyes that scanned like a soldier's. He never attended church, neither as a boy nor as a man. He didn't see the point. Life to him was a battle, not a prayer. His grandmother, a woman everyone called "Mama," raised him, and she was the only person who ever made him feel safe. But after losing her, he hardened. He didn't know what gentleness was. Not really. He raised

1

us with the toughness he needed to survive, and even though he loved us, you learned early not to mistake his love for softness.

My mother, Brenda, was softer, but not always safe. She'd lost her own mother—my grandmother Mary—to breast cancer when she was in her thirties. That kind of grief doesn't just pass—it settles. It hardens some people. It haunts others. For Brenda, it did both.

I never got to know Mary. She died when I was one. Even in still photographs, she speaks. There's one picture I've stared at for years—her smile wide and knowing, her sweater bold like her spirit, her eyes sharp but kind. She looked like a woman who didn't just walk into a room—she made it hers. There's something about her face that feels familiar. Like I inherited more than just her blood. Some of her strength seems to live within me.

That same strength showed up in my mother—but in her, it wore armor. The kind, polished daily, so no one could see the cracks. She had her own storms—addiction, heartbreak, the weight of a world that expected her to keep pushing no matter how tired she was. Yet, she moved through the world like a woman who dared it to break her again.

Brenda carried herself with undeniable flair—always posh, always put together, like she invited the world to underestimate her. Her skin was smooth and rich like sun-warmed bronze, and she often wore her hair in sharp, layered cuts that framed her face with intention. She had a radiant smile—one that could disarm you even in disappointment—and arms that held both strength and softness. Her presence filled any room she entered, dressed in bold colors and tank tops that hugged her curves, always with a hint of sparkle—whether in her earrings, her neckline, or her spirit. She was a woman who could make a statement just by sitting still.

Beneath the confidence was a woman still healing. As her daughter, I felt both the pull of her warmth and the ache of her absence—sometimes all at once.

Together, my parents were the yin and yang of my upbringing. Fire and water. Conflict and comfort. Cigarettes and short fuses. I hated the smell of smoke clinging to my hair, my clothes, my notebooks. I still do. Even now, I wouldn't trade either of them. Because somehow through it all they stayed. That is important.

I was a daddy's girl. Maybe because I couldn't fully trust my mom. I learned early that in chaos; you cling to the one person who doesn't leave. It shaped me. My voice went quieter. My shoulders carried more. I bottled things up and wore responsibility like a badge—bougie, maybe. That was my survival.

Basketball was not the dream. My desire was to be a cheerleader. I wanted to be girly. I was terrified of my own shadow. By third grade, I was already taller than most of the boys. The coaches begged. My friends insisted. So, I did both—I cheered for the boys, then played with the girls. Although I was terrible initially, something lit up in me when I stepped on that court. They needed me. Wanted me. For the first time, I felt it—the power of mattering.

That spark never left. I played until I was 26. Through losses, wins, and years that shaped my entire identity. I chased the feeling of mattering. Of being necessary. With it came a long shadow of insecurity.

* * *

CHEERED AND CHOSEN

I hated how I looked. Tall. Black. Skinny. Too dark, too confident, too fierce to be soft. I lived in a place where whiteness was the standard of beauty, and Blackness came with caveats. If you were Black, you better be light-skinned. You better have "good hair." You better be quiet and cute, not confident and bold. I didn't fit.

Boys didn't look at me. If they did, it was to laugh or whisper. My confidence and skill at sports led some to believe I was gay. They saw strength but not the loneliness behind it—the ache to be seen, not sized up.

My first boyfriend was white. He was kind. Funny. He saw me in a way no one else had. He was a senior. I was a freshman.

For weeks, he walked me to class, held my hand in the hallway, kissed me where people could see. For the first time, I wasn't invisible. He wanted me—openly. It felt dangerous and beautiful. A kind of freedom I didn't know I needed. From grade school through middle school, I had learned to tuck my crushes away like secrets. White boys didn't see me—at least not with desire. They didn't pass notes to me. Their fantasy wasn't me. I was the unnamed exception no one dared to mention.

Until him.

He kissed me as if I were worthy. Brave. Bold. Then the whispers started.

"Nigger lover." That's what they called him. Loud, in notes, hallways, lunchrooms.

After that, something in him changed. He grew quiet. Apologetic. His hand stopped reaching for mine. One day, he ended it—with a sentence so hollow I barely recognized his voice.

He didn't even look me in the eye. I told him it was okay. Though it felt like a knife, I still managed a smile.

I carried that shame home. I carried it into the shower, where I cried quietly so no one could hear. That breakup taught me what the mirror never said out loud: You're too Black to be loved without consequence.

It branded me in ways I wouldn't unpack for years. Made me question whether I'd ever be soft enough, safe enough, light enough to be chosen again.

I told no one. Not even my brother. Some heartbreak doesn't leave bruises you can point to. Just the quiet kind. The kind that teaches you how to disappear without anyone noticing.

I didn't disappear.

I worked.

School became another proving ground. I was not allowed to take AP classes. No one ever told me I was smart enough. So, I made it my mission to be undeniable. Gym rat by day. Overachiever by night. No friends. No parties. Just hoop and books.

Eventually, I grew tired of trying to fit in where I wasn't wanted. So I transferred. Left the majority-white school for a diverse one. I needed to breathe. To stop shrinking myself. At the new school, I didn't try to fit in. My face was bare. I didn't apologize for being smart. I just was.

It was here that my story started to root itself.

Coach Sonita Warren Dixon was more than a coach—she was a force. A steady, commanding presence who could light up a gym with her laugh just as easily as she could still it with her stare. She wore her power with ease, like a hoodie and sneakers—casual but undeniable. She was always moving, always observing, and always privy to more information than she disclosed.

She didn't just teach plays—she taught pride. Discipline. Emotional honesty. She was the woman who could call out your potential before you even believed in it. With her beanie pulled low, whistle hanging loose around her neck. Sonita was the blueprint for strength without coldness. Authority without ego.

She never asked us to be perfect. Just present. Just real.

When I was seventeen and the world felt loud, Sonita became my volume control. My safe place. My emotional anchor in a storm that hadn't even fully formed yet. Long before I had the language for mentorship or the need for therapy, I had Sonita—seeing me, centering me, steadying me.

We built a team that made history—three straight championships, one undefeated season. I received the honor of being named the first-ever female McDonald's All-American from my area. North Carolina Gatorade Player of the Year, recruited by every Division I school in the country. Like my twin brother Rashad before me, I chose UNC-Chapel Hill. A Full scholarship. Four years. A dream no one ever saw coming—especially not the girl who once just wanted to cheer.

Success was mine. I experienced it. But with me, I carried everything: my insecurities, my silence, my family's weight, and the voice I was just beginning to reclaim.

My family is me.

I am a daughter of pain and resilience. I am the sister who tried to save everyone. I am the girl who stayed silent when she should have screamed. The girl who hated how she looked and didn't

5

think marriage was for her. She believed no one would ever love her as she needed—until she was proven wrong.

This isn't just a tale of triumph.

This is a story of what happens when you've "had it all" and still hurt anyway.

My journey begins here.

Becoming doesn't end with a jersey or a draft. It deepens.

After the lights fade and the applause quiets, there's a different kind of proving—one no one prepares you for. The kind you do in silence. In sweatpants. In mirrors.

LEGACY IN THE MIRROR

*T*he applause had faded. The ring was on. But the shock kept coming in waves. Yet, as I crossed that graduation stage and flung my cap into the air, the real reckoning began the next morning—when the mirror stared back, unforgiving and unfiltered.

I wasn't just entering adulthood—I was inheriting a legacy.

By the time I packed for Chapel Hill, my brother Rashad had already declared for the NBA. **McDonald's All-American. NCAA Champion. First-round pick**. Tar Heel royalty. My twin in spirit, sometimes my shadow. He etched his greatness in history. Mine? Still pencil-sketched in the margins.

He called me the night before my first day on campus.

"This shit ain't gonna be easy," he said. "But it'll be yours."

It wasn't advice. It was a transfer of weight.

Our first cousin Cameron Maybin had just gone 10th in the MLB draft. Two men in my family—millionaires before twenty. Headlines. Highlights. Shoe deals. ESPN segments. Here I was, the first female McDonald's All-American from my city, headed to a campus that already bore my family's name in banners and bleachers.

I wasn't just walking into college—I was walking into a test of identity. Could I carve my name beside theirs, or would I always be the echo?

Before we ever played a game, we had to conquer the mile.

Every position had a specific time standard. Guards 6:30. Post players 6:45. Centers 7:00 minutes. Miss it? Run it again. And again. And again. If you *still* didn't make it, you got an alternate punishment—but either way, you'd pay for falling short.

The mile was my enemy.

I hated the way the track smelled at five in the morning. I hated the cold air curling down my back. And I hated the way my lungs betrayed me when I missed my time by five seconds.

I was fast. I was lean. I was capable.

But long distance didn't love me back.

Every failed attempt scraped at the perfectionist in me.

I still hear the coaches shouting through the dark —

"4:45!"

"5:15!" I could hear myself even more. "Shit, I have half a lap left. I will not make it. My shins hurt, my chest is burning, I need my damn asthma pump!" My requirement was 6:30. But my reality? 6:45—every single time.

Eventually, I changed positions. I shifted from the wing to the post. With that change came a new standard—one I could finally meet. My new time would be 6:45!

I didn't beat the mile. But I found a way to win.

That mile taught me that sometimes success isn't about shaving off seconds. It's about shifting lanes until you can run your race at full stride.

UNC felt like home; I didn't come to be comfortable. I came to be undeniable. Still, freshman year humbled me. I played in every game. Started none. My stats weren't quite—they were whispers: 5.8 points, 3.0 rebounds, 1.2 steals. I heard the doubt in silence; saw it reflected in that mirror. You're not enough. You're not him.

Even praise from coaches couldn't drown out the internal pressure.

Do more. Be more. Earn your place.

Then came January 2006—ACC Rookie of the Week. Two strong games, one small crack in the wall of doubt. Enough to taste belief. So, I doubled down. Dawn practices. Midnight film sessions. I memorized playbooks like scripture and wore fatigue like armor.

Professors knew my name because I made sure they couldn't forget it.

Meanwhile, Rashad was giving interviews, and Cameron was rounding third in the majors. I was winning titles but not headlines. My currency wasn't checks—it was sweat. Sacrifice. Silence.

Their greatness came in dollars. Mine came in grit.

By senior year, I had earned my own kind of royalty:

- 3× ACC Champion
- 2 Final Four appearances
- WBCA and Associated Press All-American Honorable Mention
- ACC All-Academic Team
- UNC Athletic Director Scholar-Athlete
- First UNC woman ever on the cover of Sports Illustrated
- 15th overall pick in the WNBA Draft—just one spot behind my brother

History had never seen that before. Siblings drafted one pick apart. Same bloodline. Same fire. Different paths.

It should've been enough.

When people said, we always knew you had it in you, the mirror still whispered: But did you know me?

We build a legacy in silence, not in applause. The hours following practice lingered. Silent nights were spent in tears. My training began each morning before sunrise. A quiet climb, unseen by others.

Even as my points per game jumped from 5.8 to 14.4 by senior year, I wasn't chasing numbers. I was chasing peace with my reflection.

I didn't want to follow greatness—I wanted to become it.

So, I stopped chasing shadows—and built something they couldn't compare.

By the time my name was called on draft night, I wasn't trying to match the men in my family anymore. I was honoring the woman I had become.

Earned.
Etched.
Unshakeable.

Still, I'd be lying if I said the ache disappeared. Even now, I sometimes wonder if the world values the work of women with the same reverence. Same grind. Same greatness. Different reward.

I know this much: Legacy is the quiet climb when no one's watching. Mine lives in study halls, early-morning sprints, and silence. In classroom ceilings and championship floors. In the courage to compete with ghosts—and come out whole.

When no one's cheering... who do you see?

That was the question I asked myself every day I wore Carolina blue. Now, as a mother, a wife, and a woman still chasing herself, I know the answer: I am the mirror. Not the reflection.

When having it all still hurts, your legacy isn't the success. It's that you're still here.

I had made it. Carved my name beside theirs. Stood tall in my own right. But success doesn't spare you from the quiet. If anything, it makes it louder.

I had trophies. A title. A legacy built on effort, not ease. Yet — I was still searching for peace.

That's the part no one tells you. The part that came for me next.

THE DISAPPEARING ACT

I thought that reaching the mountaintop would bring peace. But peace never came.

Chapter 2 ended in applause—a banner of achievements, a legacy etched in headlines. No one talks about what happens after you reach the peak—when the lights dim, the crowd goes home, and you're left staring at yourself in the mirror wondering who you are without the chase.

By the time my draft night arrived, I had already proven myself —first to the world, then to my reflection. I was the 15th overall pick in the 2009 WNBA Draft. Rashad had gone 14th to the Timberwolves 4 years prior. Me, 15th to the Lynx. One pick apart. Same city. Same bloodline. Same dream realized.

Our journeys? We never built them the same.

His legacy came with celebration. Mine came with conditions. I didn't step into the league with a team of agents or a polished image campaign. I stepped in raw and grateful—unprepared for the sharp edges of a business never built for girls like me.

There's a certain silence that follows success—when you've achieved everything that was supposed to fix the ache, and it's still there. I had been chasing greatness for so long, I never stopped to ask what came next.

What do you do when the game you love feels like a cage?

What happens when your legacy becomes a weight you carry alone?

I arrived in Minnesota with a carry-on full of uncertainty and a heart full of hope. I did not know what came next.

When I met head coach Don Zierden, his welcome was sharp-edged. "I hope you're not like your brother," he said. "We did a background check and heard nothing but good things. But, we took a big chance on you."

A "big chance?" As if I hadn't earned my name. As if I were still just my brother's shadow — a secondary character in my life. I smiled and said thank you. That's what we're taught — be professional, smile and nod. But it stung. Deep.

I was told I would be a defender and back up Seimone Augustus, one of the greatest to ever play. I was okay with that. She was a giant in our sport. That also meant my role was predetermined, limiting my potential before I even stepped onto the court.

Then, the carousel started. Right before the season opener.

Coach Zierden was gone. Jennifer Gillom stepped in — and for a while, it felt like home again. She was a player's coach. She understood us. She resembled Coach Sonita. Unfortunately, Coach Jen didn't last. The organization decided not to renew her contract after a 14-20 record.

Cheryl Reeve took over next. Brilliant, disciplined, championship-level. Different. Her energy wasn't soft or familiar — it was firm and exact. She was sharp, strategic, and expected the same from everyone on that floor—rookie or not. I learned that the hard way.

I had a habit of forgetting to take my earrings out before practice. The first time, she was nice about it—gave me a firm warning. After we'd just come off a tough road loss, she wasn't in the mood for rookie mistakes, although I was in my second year. My unaware, unprotected, overthinking self walked into the gym with those tiny silver hoops still in.

No one warned me. I should've remembered. Before I could take my spot in the drill line, I heard it:

"McCants, take them fucking earrings out—for the fifth fucking time. That's a $200 fine."

The entire gym froze. Before my fingers touched my ears, I felt them burn. It was impossible for me to be mad at her. I felt anger towards myself for such recklessness in an environment where even earrings could be seen as a sign of disrespect.

That moment wasn't about jewelry. It was about survival. Unless you were a top-five draft pick, your contract wasn't safe. We were all on day-to-day agreements. Every practice felt like an audition—and that day, I almost blew it over something stupid.

I never wore them in practice again.

I struggled.

Mentally. Emotionally. Silently.

The WNBA was a business. That aspect hadn't prepared me. I kept my bags packed. Being traded, waived, or cut was always a possibility for me. Every mistake felt like a silent death sentence. And the pay? Don't get me started.

I survived my rookie season. Year two came—and for a while, I thought maybe I was finding my rhythm. But not for long.

They traded me mid-season.

The trade broke me.

I couldn't sleep the night before it happened. Something was off. People were acting... strangely. Lighter. Nicer. Too nice. Practice that day was unusually chill—almost hollow. No real tension, but no energy either. I felt it in my bones: something was coming.

As we walked back to the locker room after practice, an assistant coach called my name. "Hey, Rashanda. Coach Reeves wants to see you when you're dressed." That was new. I'd never had a one-on-one with her before. My heart started racing. My palms went cold. I couldn't explain it — I knew.

In her office, she didn't stall. "Rashanda, you're a skilled player. We love you on this team. But this is a business, and we have to do what's best for the organization. We're trading you to the Tulsa Shock."

I don't remember what I said. I just remember the sting. The disbelief. The heat in my chest burned, refusing to be swallowed.

Traded?

My brain couldn't catch up. What did I do? Why me? Tulsa was a new franchise at the bottom of the league. Small market. No foundation. No system. It felt like exile. Like I was being sent somewhere to disappear.

Just like that—tears poured out without permission. The pain hit like a memory. Like the moment my first boyfriend told me people were calling him a "nigger lover," and he couldn't handle it. Couldn't handle me. Couldn't love me in the open.

Now here I was again—talented, loyal, all-in—and somehow still not worth keeping.

Tulsa would be my last stop. Coach Nolan Richardson was trying to reinvent the wheel. Marion Jones was on the team—yes, that Marion Jones. And everything felt chaotic. Experimental. Nothing made sense.

The worst part?

I had no agent. No one navigating my contracts. I am unprotected. Behind closed doors: The politics remain unexplained. I was just showing up, doing my job, and getting blindsided.

Truthfully? That had been the case for a while.

My first official agent, Eric, represented me during the 2011–2012 season; this would be after Tulsa. He tried. It didn't work. In sports, you must move quickly. I received an email from Erica, a representative for Bruce, my next agent. I was in transition from Eric. She had been watching quietly from afar. Her email read: *"The fact of the matter remains that someone of your caliber should not be playing in countries like Finland and Sweden... I can't understand what's happened the past few seasons after your career was going so well. Your agent just places you—they don't fight for you."*

I read it twice. Three times.

She saw what my tiredness, loyalty, and confusion had prevented me from admitting: that someone had mishandled me. That I had been put in the wrong place. That I deserved better—and didn't know how to demand it. The timing was bad for us. We

14

never got past the first signature. I had to choose between two agents Bruce or John. John won, but it felt like I lost.

My father's health had deteriorated, and emotionally, I was done. Done feeling invisible. Done feeling like the least important name on someone's roster. Every agent had bigger clients. Flashier ones. The kind they'd post about and pitch first. I wasn't that girl.

I had fallen through the cracks. Maybe, like Don Zierden hinted on day one, they presumed I was like my brother. People painted Rashad as the villain before anyone truly knew him. Judged before he ever got to speak. I felt the weight of the same projection—unearned, unfair, and heavy.

He was out in four years.

I was out in two.

An innocent, hungry athlete. Misunderstood. Undervalued. Traded like a card. Tossed like a number. I had heart. I had game. But I didn't have a champion. In this business, talent without advocacy will always leave you alone on the floor.

* * *

THE GAME BROKE ME

I smiled during interviews. Posed for pictures. But inside—I was unraveling.

Then came the off-season — year-round ball. WNBA in the summer. Overseas in the fall and winter. I didn't rest. I didn't process it. I just kept going. That's what they expected us to do. You want to make a living playing this game? Then play. Everywhere.

My first two overseas seasons were in Israel — chaotic and beautiful. Next comes Poland, followed by Finland. After that, Sweden.

It was Poland that broke something in me.

I remember walking alone to the store one afternoon. An older white woman stared me down with a kind of disgust I had never experienced. I glanced back, and she flipped me off. No words. Just hate. I pivoted right there and went home. Called my parents on Skype, shaken.

"Momma, you will not believe what just happened to me!" I spoke. "What happened, Shanda? Are you okay?" her voice shook. I told her what had happened.

I was not alright. I didn't understand how my presence could cause that kind of random reaction from a stranger. I felt unsafe.

"Momma, I think I'm going to ask to come home. I don't like it here." I said with tears in my eyes. But I delayed my request because I'm not a quitter.

That wasn't the only moment that made me question myself.

The head coach in Poland was cold—abrasive, even. He could speak English, but refused to do so around me. Every team meeting, every breakdown, every timeout—he'd rattle off instructions in Polish, then gesture for one of the girls to translate. Most of the time, they fumbled through the translation, confused or rushed, leaving me to piece together fragments like a test I never studied for. I saw the frustration on their faces—not always toward me, but toward him. Still, I felt like a burden. The outsider. The girl who didn't belong.

His refusal to address me wasn't just inconvenient—it was humiliating. I was a professional, but he made me feel remedial. Invisible. Like my presence was an inconvenience to his comfort. The more he ignored me, the more I shrank. The more I second-guessed myself. Until one day, I wasn't just foreign. I was foreign and fading.

Then, the final straw.

After an away game, our all-male coaching staff played a full pornographic movie on the team bus. I was half-asleep when the moaning started. I opened my eyes to see bodies on screen, my teammates snickering like middle schoolers. One of them leaned over and pointed at the screen with a smile. Another glanced at me, then quickly looked away, her face flushing with something that looked like shame.

I was horrified.

I didn't say much. My face, screamed. Apparently, that was enough. I called my agent that night.

"Get me out," I said.

Turns out they were already planning to release me.

That was the first time I chose myself. Even then, I knew the cost. Women who speak up in this industry get labeled. Difficult. Problematic. Damaged goods. Word travels fast in women's basketball. Your name becomes your punishment.

After Poland, I played in Finland. Then Sweden. But I was worn out. I felt like a silhouette — present, but not whole.

Basketball had saved me for so long. Now, it was holding me hostage.

I didn't quit. I survived.

Every time I looked in the mirror, the reflection looked less like a player and more like a person I was still trying to meet.

I had given the game my body. My time. My innocence. My silence. Now, it was time to find my voice. Even if I didn't yet know how to use it.

Sometimes, healing doesn't start with hope. Sometimes, it starts with loss.

Before I could step into the next version of myself, life would strip away the one identity I had always clung to:

The athlete.

WHEN TELLING THE TRUTH
COST YOU EVERYTHING

I never planned to stop playing basketball.

I thought the game would carry me longer—long enough to retire on my own terms: stronger, richer, and ready. But sometimes life makes the choice for you, and it doesn't ask for your approval.

After Sweden, my last team, I returned home to find my father noticeably weaker. He looked smaller somehow, like the man who had raised me was folding into himself. I had seen this coming. We all had. The diabetes, the swelling, the fatigue—it wasn't new. What was new was the word they attached to it now: end-stage kidney failure. A diagnosis that doesn't just change your plans—it rearranges your reality.

He needed dialysis four times a week. Each session took three to four hours. He couldn't consume over 24 ounces of liquid per day. That was hell for a man who loved water. He drank it like oxygen. Now, what gave him life could also take it.

In that moment, I knew—I couldn't leave him again.

The last time I had to say goodbye, it was to my grandfather. I was playing in Finland. He passed away while I was under contract, and when I asked to fly home, the club said no. My salary couldn't cover the flight myself. So, I said goodbye on a screen. Sat in a quiet room, holding a laptop, staring at a man who had already gone cold.

My grandfather had a presence that couldn't be taught. He dressed sharp enough to turn heads and warm enough to make strangers feel like family, he moved through the world with a kind of ease that made you feel safer just being near him. He didn't speak loudly to be heard—his spirit did that for him. In his Sunday best—white suit, gold tie, matching pocket square, hat tilted just right—he looked like joy dressed in elegance. But it was the glimmer in his eye that lingered most. The one that said, *I've got stories to tell and love to give while I do it.*

Losing him that way, not being allowed to say goodbye properly, was a grief that burned a hole in my chest—a memory I swore I would never repeat.

So, I made the choice. No more planes. No more contracts. No more running. I was done.

What now?

Basketball was my language, my schedule, my therapy, my income. Without it, I was just... floating. I don't float. I sink—into purpose. If I didn't find one soon, I knew I'd drown.

So, I entered the automotive industry.

It wasn't glamorous; it was loud and fast-paced and full of people who didn't care about jump shots or stat lines. I had to learn a new game, a new playbook—and quickly. There was something steadying about it. The business side of cars taught me more about human nature than any locker room ever had.

In sales, you learn to listen before you speak. You learn to hold space for people who carry more than they say. You learn to read tone. Body language. Silence. Most importantly, you learn compassion. I saw my value not just in what I could sell, but in how I made people feel.

I became the person others came to for answers—even strangers. I stood out not just because I was different, but because I made people feel safe. "You have a calming presence," they'd say. I didn't always feel that way on the inside, but I took the compliment.

Still, the pressure never left me. Even though I was done with the sport, my inner voice hadn't quit.

"Do more." "Be better." "They need more from you." "You're not doing enough."

No matter how much I achieved, I always felt like I was failing someone. My family. Myself. The younger version of me who thought being great would make everything easier.

* * *

WHEN TRUTH GOT ME SPIT ON

Then came the scandal.

It started with a quiet conversation—one that made the air in the room feel colder than it was. Mary Willingham, someone I knew and deeply respected at UNC, shared her concerns with me. She had uncovered something massive, something wrong.

My brother confirmed it.

Academic fraud.

Classes that didn't exist.

Grades that weren't earned.

Degrees handed out like performance bonuses.

I was floored.

If you've read my story this far, you know how hard I worked for every grade. I was more than just an athlete. I prided myself on being a scholar. I was a State Farm All-American. ACC All-Academic Team. UNC Athletic Director's Scholar-Athlete. Those awards were mine because I earned them—I had to believe that.

So, to find out I may have been part of a system that robbed me of that truth—without my knowledge—was a betrayal I still don't have words for. It shook me to my core. Everything I had stood for suddenly had a crack down the middle.

"Did I really earn what I thought I did? Was I just another name on a list?"

My brother used to call me a square. Lovingly, of course. I always obeyed the rules. I did not cheat. I did not take any shortcuts. I was the "do it right even if it takes longer" kind of person. So, when I realized how deep the deception went—and how few people would speak up—I felt like I had no choice. If I stayed silent, I was complicit.

So, I joined the lawsuit.

We wanted justice.

We got backlash.

I didn't expect applause. I also didn't expect spit.

It was March Madness 2016. I had just finished a long shift and grabbed dinner with colleagues. It was late, but the streets were still buzzing. After we said our goodbyes, I walked alone to my car. I remember being tired but content, relieved finally to have a quiet moment for myself.

That's when I heard it.

A man's voice from behind me—loud, angry.

"You stupid bitch!"

I turned slowly. Surely he wasn't talking to me.

He was.

Before I could react, I felt it.

Spit.

Hot, wet, violent. Right on my face.

He ran.

I froze.

My body wanted to chase him, scream, hit something. But it wouldn't move. Fear paralyzed me—not just fear, but also the weight of why. Why me? Why now? Why did telling the truth feel like being hunted?

I'm glad I didn't chase him. Because anything could've been waiting around that corner.

The damage was already done.

I got in my car—hands shaking, throat tight—and cried the cry you don't post about. The kind that lives in the silence between heartbeats.

When I finally spoke up, it didn't bring justice. It brought spit.

I didn't want spit.

I wanted truth.

And truth, as I'd just learned, is rarely safe—especially when it's a Black woman's. I drove away shaken, my spirit splintered but still standing. I didn't know it then, but that moment wasn't just an ending.

It was a reckoning.

Not long after, I met the man who would steady my steps. He would remind me what peace could feel like again. But before I could receive peace, I had to face what silence had taken from me.

Not the kind of silence you choose.

The kind that chooses you—when the world makes it clear that your truth costs too much.

I didn't lose my voice that night.

I buried it.

Like before... I disappeared inside my own skin.

PRESSURE, PEACE, AND THE MAN WHO SAW ME

*A*fter the spit, I went quiet again.

Not out loud—but somewhere deeper. The quiet that doesn't silence your voice, just your ability to speak. I didn't tell anyone right away, not even the people I loved. The day after it happened, I stood in my bathroom mirror and stared at my reflection, willing myself not to cry. I had spent my entire life being told, directly and indirectly, that silence was safer than truth. That telling only made things worse. So, I held it in—again. I swallowed the lump in my throat, just like that little girl who stopped going to church, who stopped trusting, who let the weight of *say nothing or you'll get in trouble* shape her silence.

It was happening all over again.

I was twenty-eight, and I felt nine—small, unprotected, and afraid to make a sound.

The betrayal didn't stop with the man who spat on me. That was just the most visible violation. The deeper cuts came from teammates, friends, fans—people I once thought would show up for me when it mattered most. People I once shared dreams with. They all fell away. No calls. No texts. Not even a "you good?"— just silence, like I had become invisible overnight. It felt like losing everyone at once. It felt like grief.

23

Some of that silence had started long before the spit. After the lawsuit. After I told the truth.

Teammates who had once shared locker rooms with me, laughed with me, broken bread with me—gone.

Not even a word. Not even a question.

Their distance wasn't just silence. It was confirmation. That telling the truth, even when it cost you everything, meant you no longer belonged.

Still—I kept going.

I had no choice.

Survival had become second nature by then—checking the mail with a tight chest, juggling overdue notices like puzzle pieces, praying one check would clear before the next crisis hit.

One afternoon, I was sitting at the end of the couch with my knees pressed to my chest, scrolling through my bank account with dread in my throat. My phone buzzed.

"Yo, I need your help," Rashad said.

"With what?" I asked, though I already knew. "I need to hold some cash. I thought this China gig would finalize this week, but there are delays. I thought I would have the money upfront and that would cover it, but—"

I looked up at the ceiling, like maybe God would drop a miracle through the drywall. I didn't have the money either. Not really. But I'd find it. "I'll figure it out," I said.

He paused. "You always do. I'll get it right back to you once this money hits."

I hung up and stared at the chipped edge of the coffee table, rage pressing behind my ribs. Not at him. Not even with my family. At the fact that I was still the only safety net any of us had.

From 2014 to 2016, I was the only steady paycheck in my entire family. After five years of waiting and waiting for the NBA to call, my brother had fallen—hard. His world had gone from red carpets and champagne rooms to negative balances and broken promises. The fall was so steep, none of us saw it coming until the elevator hit the basement and the lights went out. We had been in free fall and didn't even know it.

I was paying rent for a four-bedroom residential rental home that now held our entire family—my mom, my dad, my sister, and her two babies. My brother sold his custom-built home. The dream we built our futures around. It was gone—faded like a banner after the parade ends. My cousin Cameron and Aunt Renee helped when they could—God bless them—but the financial burden fell mostly on me. Rent, food, bills. Life. I carried it all, while my brother picked up occasional gigs and my sister remained inconsistent, always on the edge of another emergency.

She was still figuring herself out—had been since she was sixteen. Two kids by twenty, still no real anchor. I loved her, but I was drowning trying to be her life raft.

By April 2016, I couldn't do it anymore.

Something in me snapped—not in anger, but in self-preservation. I remember sitting at the kitchen table and telling them all, "I'm moving out in June." My voice cracked. Guilt clawed at my insides. But I had to choose me—maybe for the first time in my life. And choosing yourself, especially in a family full of survivors, feels like betrayal wrapped in freedom. I needed to safeguard the undamaged parts of myself.

Of course, I couldn't leave without setting things up first. I found a lease for my parents. I called Aunt Renee in Asheville and asked her to help Sade. She found a trailer in our hometown. I mapped out everything because that's what I did—I planned everyone's escape but my own. Until now.

Sade got evicted from that trailer. Sade's eviction did not surprise me—but it still hurt. Then came another rescue mission. This time, it wasn't mine alone. Aunt Renee and I pleaded with Cameron—our family's second twin flame—to help. He did. He paid for two years of prepaid rent and bought her a car in cash. A full reset. My mother, the Queen of Hair, became the legacy. Sade, now doing hair too, was supposed to be set. What came next? That's her story to tell.

For me—it was the first time I let go.

Letting go gave me space to be me again.

June 15th was move-in day. My apartment smelled like new

beginnings. That fresh-paint-meets-freedom scent that only comes when a space is finally yours. I spent hours arranging, decorating, and organizing—every pillow fluffed just right, every kitchen cabinet labeled and aligned. My little OCD heart was at peace.

The bed was brand new. I'd picked it out myself—firm mattress, deep gray headboard, wrapped in silence and soft sheets. A 65-inch TV hung proudly across the room — too big for the space, but perfect for the life I was building.

I poured a glass of red wine, barefoot, still in leggings, and sank into the couch like it could hold everything I had just let go of. Voices are absent. No demands. There is no one calling my name. Just me.

I looked around, took in every inch of my new world, and whispered to myself:

"You deserve this. You earned this. Don't take this away from us."

The "us" wasn't royal. It was plural. It was me and the little girl I used to be. The one who used to hold it all in. The one who always made room for everyone else. Tonight, she finally had a room of her own.

I didn't go wild—I'm not wired like that. But I dated, I laughed, I dressed up, I slept in. I reclaimed pieces of myself I didn't know were missing.

Then—I met Chris.

It was his birthday. A friend-of-a-friend invitation. One of those nights you almost cancel—but don't. The introduction shifted something between us. It wasn't fireworks or slow-motion music. It was quiet certainty. Sparks didn't fly—they settled. Soft. Quiet. Familiar. Like we'd known each other in a life before this one.

He wore a soft coral polo that brought out the warmth in his skin, with the top buttons undone like someone comfortable with who he was. A sleek black watch wrapped his wrist, and behind his glasses, his eyes held a calm that made everything around him feel less chaotic. He didn't try very hard—and yet he was unforgettable.

He arrived with no intention of fixing anything or saving me. Fully himself, he just stood there. Grounded. Gentle. Respectful. Different. And I noticed.

From that moment on, things changed.

I did not know I'd marry him. Initially, marriage seemed like an impossibility to me. I'd built such high walls that I had given up on finding a way out. Chris didn't knock—he waited until I invited him in. When I did, he stayed.

The ring, the shock, and everything in between? That's coming.

This chapter, this version of me—was the first time I chose me.

That decision made love possible.

When love arrived—it didn't crash in like lightning. It moved like light. Quiet. Certain. Warm in all the places I thought had gone cold.

Chris didn't rescue me.

He recognized me.

THE RAINBOW AFTER THE STORM

*C*hris was unlike anyone I'd ever known—exactly what I needed without realizing it. The man who didn't interrupt your silence but sat inside it with you.

He stayed in his own lane. Quiet but present. Humble, but confident in a way that didn't need to be loud. When we met, I was finally living on my own, decorating my apartment the way I liked it. That was my moment of peace. Of arrival. Of choosing myself.

Then—Chris.

He had his own place, drove a black Camaro, and worked in the car business too. We connected quickly—on more than surface-level things. Our moms share the same birthday. A coincidence that felt like foreshadowing. Our fathers both had military backgrounds. We were both middle children with two siblings. He's the only boy from his mom. My brother is the only boy from my mom. Our mothers came from big families, too—five siblings or more.

I hadn't met his parents yet, but from the way he spoke about them, I could tell they mattered. His mom, Sheila, had a bold, vibrant energy—always well-dressed, full of spirit, and never shy about her faith. His dad, Big Chris, was quiet but solid, a steady presence with a strength that didn't need to announce itself. The way they raised him explained so much about who he was—grounded, thoughtful, steady. Safe.

It felt like we'd grown up on opposite ends of the same street—parallel lives shaped by different houses but the same foundation. Now, here we were. Aligned.

What caught me wasn't our similarities. It was that he saw me —not my résumé, not my basketball legacy, not the weight I carried or the people I was trying to save. Just me. Rashanda.

He was buying his first home. I was still renting my first apartment. Yet—he started saying "we."

He would ask where "we" should put the bed, how "we" might set up the living room, or how many couches "we" might need. At first, I was confused. I told my mom about it, and she smiled in that mother-knows-everything way and said,

"Shanda, he's building a future with you in his mind. He's including you in his plans."

I was so oblivious. Like, why would he do that? This is his house. He's paying the mortgage. I would never just be here living off him.

That's when the self-talk crept in again. Try not to be a burden. Remain vigilant. Don't rely on anyone. That was the script I'd memorized. That was the cost of strength in a world that taught me to carry everything without asking for help. This time—my heart and mind disagreed.

I let him love me first. I let myself love him back.

We went on dates to the zoo, walked past giraffes like old friends, ate overpriced pizza, laughed about nothing and watch Wrestling on Monday nights. He came with me to Las Vegas for my 30th birthday—no pressure, no performance. Just presence. We were inseparable. Wherever he went, I was close by. And if I wasn't, he noticed. I needed him in a way I never thought I could. And he wanted me. That was new to me.

* * *

THE LOSS WE NEVER SPOKE OF

By February, everything changed.

I was still living in my apartment when I took that test. Alone. I remember standing in the bathroom, holding the stick, staring at the result as if it had betrayed me.

Pregnant.

The word looked louder than it felt. My body stayed still, but my mind sprinted—through fear, through disbelief, through a thousand imagined futures I hadn't prepared for.

I went to Chris's townhouse that night. He was watching wrestling on the couch in the loft. I sat beside him, quiet. Processing. Then, I used the same line I'd use again later.

"Chris, I lost my period."

He looked up at me with that sarcastic grin I'd grown to love.

"You better find her ass."

I laughed. A real one—short, sharp, like air rushing out of something that had been too full. Then I cried. Not from panic, but from possibility. From how unready and yet how right it felt.

We were both in shock. We didn't know what this meant, or what we were supposed to do. He got quiet—the way calm people do when the world shifts beneath their feet. Not withdrawn, just inward. I didn't need words. I just needed him to stay. And he did.

The next few weeks were a blur of emotion and nervous planning. We had our first ultrasound appointment—Chris came with me, sat right beside me during the vaginal ultrasound. The room was dim and sterile, and I was nervous but excited.

The technician was quiet.

I thought nothing of it—I saw the little image on the screen, that tiny life beginning to bloom. I was smiling so hard it hurt.

The room remained quiet.

We never heard a heartbeat.

The technician pulled the wand out gently and said, "She'll be right back. When she returned, she told me to get dressed and follow her. She led us into a small office that felt like death—cold, silent.

The doctor wasn't even there in person. A voice came through the speakerphone, clinical and distant. Before the words landed, there was a pause—just long enough to give me hope.

"I'm sorry. This is common. You can try again. It's nothing you did," she said, her tone soft but practiced, like someone trying to sound human through a script.

I heard nothing after that. Just the hum of the speaker and the quiet ache of something leaving me before I ever got to hold it.

She offered me two options—surgical removal or a pill. I chose the pill. Fewer complications, they said.

While waiting to check out, I lost it.

I broke down in a way I didn't know I could. Sobbing uncontrollably. I was always the anchor, holding everything together, but now I am broken. Chris held me in the middle of that waiting room while I crumbled. To be fair, I know a part of him crumbled too.

The pill took hours to kick in. When it did, the pain was like nothing I'd ever felt before. I curled into a ball on the floor, wearing a diaper, shaking from the cramps and disbelief. And when it happened—when my body passed what I could only describe as a large, blood-covered sac—I knew what it was.

That was my baby.

I'll never forget it. I'll never unsee it.

The grief came in waves. Still does sometimes. The guilt. The questions. The loneliness. What soothed me the most came the same day.

Chris looked at me with eyes full of love and sorrow and asked, "Do you want to try again?" Not as a solution. Not as a fix. But as a promise. That we could rebuild something beautiful out of something that shattered us. I cried all over again. "Yes."

Two months later, I noticed the signs again. The weird feelings. The late period. This time, I knew.

Chris was watching wrestling again on the couch. I stood in the doorway, heart racing.

"Chris, I lost my period."

He didn't even blink.

"You better find her ass," he said with familiarity, and a full-faced smile. I laughed—and then I cried.

Terrified.

Thankful.

In awe.

This was our rainbow baby. Our second chance. Our beginning. This time—we faced it the way we always did. **Together.**

Just as new life took root in me—another life I loved was slipping. It's wild how joy and fear don't take turns. They arrive together. Like breath and heartbeat. Like love and loss.

I didn't know it yet, but the next call would remind me — **peace doesn't mean the pressure stops.**

A RING, A KIDNEY, AND EVERYTHING IN BETWEEN

I remember exactly where I was when my father called. I was standing in the kitchen barefoot, holding a half-washed dish when my phone buzzed.

"Goldie," he said—his voice steady, but something trembled underneath. "I got good news."

Just like that, I forgot how to breathe.

"They found a donor. I'm getting a kidney transplant. October 9th."

Everything inside me froze.

It was supposed to be good news. It was good news. But fear didn't care. It rose anyway, sudden and sharp, curling around my ribs like a warning.

I was still grieving the miscarriage. Still hovering, obsessing, praying over the new pregnancy growing inside me. Now I had a new terror: the fear that saving him might be the very thing that took him from me.

He had been deteriorating for months. Dialysis was keeping him alive but not living. He wasn't himself anymore. Not fully. I had watched him shrink. In body, in energy, in will. We were running out of time. I had never dared to say it out loud.

My father wasn't a man of faith. Never had been. "God"

wasn't someone you'd hear him thank. So, I did it for him. Quietly. Desperately. Repeatedly.

Don't take my dad, please. Let him meet this baby. Let him stay with me, please. He's always been here. Please don't change that now.

I whispered it until it turned into a prayer he wouldn't ask for. A plea stitched together from memories, fear, and love too big to carry silently. I said it anyway.

Somehow—he made it through.

We made it through.

The surgery was a success. I got my father back. Not all of him —he moved slower now, rested more. But the core? Still in one piece. Still mine. Still calling me Goldie like I was five, and he was still invincible.

Just weeks later, we celebrated life in the biggest way possible: my baby shower.

The theme was perfect—pink and gold, soft and radiant. Like joy made visible. Roses spilled across tabletops; ribbons curled like laughter in the air.

My aunt Renee made magic that day. She wasn't just the host —she was the architect of an atmosphere I didn't even know I needed. Everything she touches has a kind of effortless grace to it, like she can see the celebration before it exists. Renee has always been that way—sharp-eyed, soft-spoken, with a smile that says, "I got this" even when the world is crumbling.

She walked in with her signature glasses perched perfectly, her hair flawless, and a quiet glow that filled the room before the decorations did. The candles, the colors, the comfort—it was all hers. She didn't just organize an event; she wrapped love around every inch of that space. She made sure every detail whispered, *you're worthy of this joy.*

That day, she wasn't just my aunt. She was my calm. My coordinator. My quiet strength in heels. In that moment, as I stood there glowing and anxious and swollen with both love and life, I knew—Aunt Renee had created a memory I'd carry forever.

My stylist styled my hair in long braids. My dress hugged my belly in soft lavender. Everything about me glowed.

Even my father—normally cool and composed—couldn't hold back. Just moments before the big surprise, he cried. Big, heavy tears. The kind he'd only ever held before. His baby girl was becoming a mother. The man standing beside her had already asked for her father's blessing.

He knew. And almost gave it away.

Chris stood beside me like a quiet anchor, steady in the storm of my emotions. He didn't need to say much. His presence was the sentence. His love was the punctuation. He laughed with our guests, greeted my family, rubbed my back when I waddled instead of walked.

As the shower wound down and guests started to leave, Chris made a small gesture — he asked for everyone's attention.

His voice was shaky but determined.

"Thanks everyone for coming. I have a gift for Rashanda and Reya," he said.

His smile was big—but his nerves were louder. They clung to the corners of his eyes, made his voice shake just enough to give him away.

He handed me a gift bag—soft pink, stuffed with tissue paper. Everyone stared.

I looked at him, confused.

A gift? From him?

I opened it slowly, wondering what he'd come up with. Is it a photo? Is it a letter? Is it a bracelet?

No, it was a onesie. A tiny, delicate, pink baby onesie folded into itself like a secret.

I lifted it out and unfolded it.

There, in white letters across the chest, it read:

"Mommy, will you marry Daddy?"

I froze.

My breath caught. My heart tumbled into my stomach. I covered my mouth with both hands and dropped my head into them.

Tears poured out of me. Loud. Unstoppable. The entire room held its breath.

Marriage was never in my plans. Not for me. Not in this life. But suddenly, I couldn't imagine anything more right. More possible.

"YES," I sobbed. "Absolutely yes."

Everyone clapped. Cheered. Cried. Just like that—I was no longer just someone's mother-to-be. I was somebody's fiancée.

Then, in true Rashanda fashion, I gave him the wrong hand.

In the middle of my overwhelmed daze, I stuck out my right hand instead of my left. Chris, just as nervous as I was, didn't even notice. He slid the ring on.

It fit—but barely.

Minutes later, my finger throbbed. The clapping continued, but panic set in. My pregnant fingers were swelling around the band.

Then I heard my Aunt Michelle shout, "It's on the wrong hand!" I instantly looked down, still not fully understanding, and fell into my throned chair. "It's on the wrong hand, damn!!!"

We laughed it off at first.

Everyone was offering solutions—thread, lotion, prayers—but nothing worked. The ring was stuck, and it was turning into a scene.

"I'll fix it later," I promised. "Let's just finish the shower."

By the time we got home, I could barely think straight. My body was completely exhausted. My feet ached. My back was seizing up. My finger was now a shade of purple I didn't know existed.

"Babe... we might have to cut it off," I whispered.

I didn't know if I meant the ring or the finger.

We turned to YouTube, desperate. The solution. Windex.

I watched as Chris grabbed the bottle from under the sink and went to work. He sprayed; I winced. He pulled. I cried. He tried again. I cried harder.

Finally—after a fourth spray and a last, determined tug—the ring slid off.

I collapsed in relief.

We both just sat there, looking at the ring in his hand. Still perfect. Still whole. Just like us.

My heart was split wide open. This was love. Not the pretty version. Not the effortless kind. The authentic kind. The kind you must work for. Fight through. Cry over. Survive with.

It had all come at once—life, loss, hope, fear, love, family, the future.

This is when "When Having It All Still Hurts" truly took shape. Even as I held everything I had ever wanted in one hand, the other was still sore from where it had nearly been taken from me.

I thought having it all would finally let me exhale. But wholeness isn't always weightless. Sometimes the deepest ache comes after the miracle.

No one prepares you for how much of your body, your identity, your peace—will fracture quietly beneath the beauty.

THE DAY I BECAME TWO PEOPLE

*T*he baby shower had glittered. The proposal stunned. The ring stuck—like magic you don't question for fear it might vanish. But life doesn't hold its sparkle for long—not in the raw, holy, unfiltered realm of motherhood.

December came fast.

I was swollen, exhausted, and wobbling under the weight of it all—my body, my emotions, my nerves. My dad was home recovering from a life-saving kidney transplant, and I was holding on to the belief that he'd live long enough to hold my daughter. I whispered prayers he never asked for. I was doing everything I could to keep peace within me. Even joy can be heavy—especially when it's layered with grief, hope, and a body that no longer feels entirely your own.

Then it happened.

It started in the middle of the night.

I was lying in bed, listening to the quiet breath of a sleeping house when the first wave of pressure gripped me—low, deep, and certain. I sat up, blinked in the dark, and waited. Another contraction came—closer this time. I stood, began pacing the room, and opened the contraction timer app on my phone. They were coming fast—every few minutes.

I hesitated for a second, then leaned over and gently woke Chris.

"Babe... I think it's time."

He stirred and sat up instantly, calm as always. I could feel his nerves humming under the surface, but he didn't let them show. He grabbed the bag, helped me into my shoes, and we drove to Duke Regional Hospital in the quiet dark of early morning. No traffic, no delay. Just streetlights blinking like metronomes. The sound of our tires and the quiet tremor of pain rippled through me with every bump. I squeezed my eyes shut, bracing between waves.

At the hospital, they checked me—four centimeters. Not enough for the epidural yet.

I nodded, trying to stay calm. Then, out of nowhere, I lurched forward and vomited—hard. A nurse quickly steadied me, wiped my mouth, and offered a basin. I felt embarrassed. Exposed. Like my body was betraying me before I had even stepped into the role of mother.

"I'm so sorry," I whispered.

She smiled kindly. "It's okay, miss. Your body's doing the work."

Still, I begged for relief. "Please... can I get the epidural?"

"Soon," she said. "Once you hit five."

Chris never left my side. Holding my hand. Watching. Silent and present. His steadiness was the only thing in the room that didn't move.

When I finally hit five centimeters, they called in the anesthesiologist. I sat hunched forward, clutching a pillow, while they slid the needle into my spine. Within minutes, the pain softened, and the world became bearable again.

My mom and mother-in-law arrived, both of them glowing with love and worry. Time passed in waves until the nurse came in to check me again—and paused.

"It's time," she said.

There was no doctor in the room yet. Just her.

She guided me into position and told me to push.

One.

Two.

She quickly stepped back, alarmed.

"Stop. Stop pushing! The baby's coming fast—too fast."

She hit the call button. Moments later, the door swung open. The doctor entered mid-hustle, gloves snapping on. I didn't know him. I wouldn't know him if I passed him in a grocery store today. But for that one moment, he was the most important man in the room. The stranger who caught my daughter. The stranger who witnessed my transformation.

With the third push, Reya entered the world. With her arrival, a version of me vanished—replaced by someone new. Mother. Witness. Warrior.

I didn't get to hold her right away. She had swallowed meconium, and they rushed her to the side to check her breathing.

I craned my neck. My heart pounded. I couldn't see what was happening—only the backs of nurses and blue gloves moving fast.

Then came the words that brought me back to life:

"She's okay."

They placed her in my arms—tiny, warm, perfect. She blinked up at me, and I broke wide open.

That's when the bleeding began.

The doctor's face turned serious. Focused. He called for more gauze.

The tear from my clitoris to my anus traumatized me beyond my expectations. The kind no one warned me about.

Tiny tears. Everywhere.

"I've seen nothing like this before," the doctor muttered.

He stitched me for forty-five straight minutes—gloved hands trembling, sweat beading across his forehead. The room kept filling with nurses, one after the other, all bringing more gauze, more light, more pressure.

They pressed, packed, applied pressure. The bleeding wasn't stopping. The room went quiet except for the hum of urgency.

My mom and mother-in-law stood stunned. Chris was pale, watching every move but saying nothing. My body had given life —and was now fighting not to give up its own.

Eventually, they stabilized me. But it took everything. Two blood transfusions. Countless stitches. Every ounce of strength I didn't know I had.

I was tired in a way sleep couldn't fix.

I didn't cry. I didn't speak. I just gazed at Reya's face while holding her. I had to memorize it. Just in case.

In that delivery room, under fluorescent lights and with a body broken open, I became someone new. I became two people.

Rashanda.

And Reya's mother.

Nothing would ever be the same again.

The days that followed blurred into each other—feedings, healing, family visits, learning how to hold a baby and hold myself together at the same time.

I smiled. I powered through. Somewhere between changing diapers and answering texts with heart emojis, I stopped checking in with the woman who had just survived it all.

I didn't fall apart.

I faded.

In that slow unraveling, something deeper began to stir—a quiet knowing that wouldn't go away. I had become two people.

Now, one of them was slipping through my fingers. I didn't know it yet, but I was about to find my way back to her.

LICENSE TO RECLAIM

$\mathcal{T}$he days folded into each other. I kept showing up—
nursing, burping, giving everything I had.

Breastfeeding Reya was one of the most beautiful—and most
brutal—acts of devotion I've ever known. I was determined to do
it, but nothing about it came easy. The postpartum pain was so
severe I needed opioids just to move. That meant pumping and
dumping. Formula feedings laced with guilt. My supply barely
held up. My confidence, even less.

We co-slept with Reya—not because people advised it, but
because it was the only way we could keep going. Reya slept on my
chest. I fed her in the same position, heart to heart, barely blinking
through the fear that something could go wrong. A blanket shifting. Chris rolling over. Every moment held its own quiet panic.

Breastfeeding demanded everything: my time, my body, my
mind. It tethered me to love and survival at once. I pushed through
months of exhaustion and self-doubt, convinced that stopping
would make me less of a mother.

But Reya was thriving—eating solids, sleeping longer,
adjusting with ease. I was still nursing her when I finally let myself
exhale.

She was five months old when I sat on the edge of the couch—

bottle in one hand, baby toy in the other—wearing a tank top that had become both uniform and armor. The sun peeked through the blinds as it always did. But that day, it didn't feel warm. It just felt... routine.

With wide, curious eyes and kicking legs, Reya was oblivious to the growing silence within me as I looked at her.

My love for her was immense. I adored Chris. I loved our life. I didn't recognize myself. Not just the body I'd carried before pregnancy—but the fire. The vision. The woman who dreamed out loud.

I wasn't the woman who could sit still in a pretty house forever, playing background to everyone else's growth. I had given birth, bled, healed, breastfed, and sacrificed, yet my desire to build remained. My intention was to contribute. Not just financially.

I wanted my name back—the one I'd earned, not inherited. Not the name that came with diapers and dishes, but the one that came with drive and dreams.

Going back into the car business made little sense anymore. Those hours, that grind—it would've gutted the home we were trying to create. We needed two incomes, but we also needed peace. Balance. Stability.

That's when the voice returned—the one from the backseat of my childhood, yelling "bingo!" at houses that looked like castles. Believing one day I'd claim one of my own.

Real estate.

The dream had been sitting quietly in the back of my mind, waiting for its cue.

I whispered it to myself the first time like a question: "Could I really do this?"

Chris didn't hesitate when I pitched him the idea. "You'd be great at it," he said. "People trust you. You care. You know homes like the back of your hand."

That was all I needed.

I enrolled in the 75-hour real estate course, nervous but ready. Reya was still nursing, and time was scarce—but I carved it out. I studied during naps, logged hours at night, and carried flashcards like a lifeline.

Then... I failed.

Missed passing by **two points**.

I sat in the parking lot afterward, hands on the wheel, completely still. The tears came before I could stop them. Chris's name lit up my phone, like he already knew. I answered without a word.

"Hey," he said gently. I sniffed. "I missed it. I failed. I have to retake the whole thing. I don't know if I can do this again."

Silence.

Then Chris said, "You came this far. Why give up now?" His voice didn't carry pity. Just presence. Belief. The belief I hadn't found in myself yet.

"I feel like a fraud," I admitted. "Like I talked all this big talk and I can't even pass a test. Twice."

Chris took a breath. "Babe. That test doesn't define you. You've passed harder things in life. Way harder. You're not failing —you're figuring it out."

His words filled my ears as I closed my eyes. I wanted to believe him. I wanted to believe I still had what it took to start over.

"You really think I can do this?" I whispered.

"I know you can," he said. "And I'll be right here—again and again—until you do." He didn't push. He pulled—back to belief. Back to why I started.

I could feel his steadiness through the phone. He had the same quiet fire I'd always had on the court. Maybe that's why we found each other.

Chris had played for Saint Augustine's University, a historic HBCU, with pride and legacy in every brick. He'd won championships, led a team. He knew how it felt to want to quit right before the win.

"I don't want to waste anymore money."

"You're not wasting anything," he said. "You're learning. This is your next season."

I signed up again.

Paid the full fee. Logged every hour. Took every quiz. This time, I asked more questions. I let go of the fear of looking unsure —because pretending to know everything had never helped me grow.

I stopped pretending I wasn't tired and started reminding myself:

Tired doesn't mean incapable.

Tired doesn't mean you quit.

It just means you rest—and rise anyway.

When the final exam came, I passed. Then I passed the national and state exams.

When I received my official certificate—after all the hours, hormones, doubts, and delays—I cried like I'd won a title.

Because I had.

I was a mother now, yes. A wife. A homemaker. But I was also still *me*—competitive, driven, and capable of building something from scratch.

That real estate license wasn't just a new career. It was a reclaiming. Of my voice. My confidence. My identity.

The license was only the beginning. By month three, I was grinding—prospecting, making calls, staring at a blank database that mocked me. Everyone seemed to "know" me, but I realized how few people I truly knew. Being an introvert in a business built on people felt like stepping onto a court where I didn't know the plays. My start was slow, and the silence was heavy.

The weight of the past still clung to me. I didn't know who had spit on me, and every stranger I met felt like they could carry that same hate. On top of that, there was mom guilt—ugly and relentless. Every hour I spent trying to build my career felt like an hour I was missing Reya's milestones. Was she safe? Was she okay? My brain was fogged by anxiety, but I kept moving because stopping wasn't an option.

Then, out of nowhere, a lifeline. A good friend from the car business called. He and his wife were ready to buy their first home —and they wanted me. Me. I was equal parts terrified and determined. I didn't know everything yet, but I knew how to outwork anyone, and I knew how to fight for people.

After signing a buyer agency agreement with me we were ready to roll. I set them up on a search; I set myself up on a search and got to work. Two weeks later, they called: "We found the house."

I sprang into action, researching every detail of the neighborhood, preparing every document. The sellers were investors, and I learned fast—they only cared about the bottom line. But that didn't scare me. The car business had already taught me how to negotiate when everyone's cards were on the table.

We went under contract. My first client. My first win. It felt better than beating Duke on their home court again.

I learned real estate isn't a straight line. The inspection revealed a nightmare—ductwork in the crawlspace that looked like a horror scene: wet, broken, a mess. I barely knew what ductwork even meant, but I learned quickly. My clients wanted it fixed. The sellers refused.

That was my moment. My test. I didn't get into this business for the money—I got in because I love helping people, and I wasn't about to let my clients down. I negotiated until we found a solution. Both the listing agent and I took a $1,500 cut from our commissions to cover the repairs. We closed two weeks later.

My first check was smaller than I'd imagined, but my pride was bigger than any paycheck. I didn't strike out on my first at-bat.

Still, after all the adrenaline, all the lessons learned, I came home and put on my other hat: Mommy. I swallowed my anxiety, picked up Reya, and reminded myself why I was fighting so hard.

Motherhood didn't erase my ambition—it just made it more urgent. In that urgency, I found purpose again.

The girl who had always wanted more?

She was back. This time, she had a license to prove it. With it came something new — not just belief in myself... but the freedom to imagine more.

More space. More peace. More room to dream beyond survival.

This wasn't about starting over.
It was about *building forward*.

THE MOTHER I THOUGHT I'D BE

e thought we were just house hunting. But really, we were vision casting—mapping out a life we hadn't fully spoken aloud yet. Dreaming with our feet on the ground and our hearts wide open.

It started small—late-night Zillow scrolling and open house weekends that felt more like dates. Chris had just received another promotion, and I had just passed my real estate exams. We were growing—together. Not just as individuals, but as a unit. Our family. Our careers. Our dreams. All of it was stretching, strengthening, and suddenly, our little townhome in Durham felt like a pair of shoes Reya had outgrown—filled with memories, but snug in all the wrong places. Still precious, but no longer a fit.

We loved the new construction homes. There's something magical about watching a home go from blueprint to beams to brick—something symbolic about building from the ground up. Our townhome had been that. And now, we wanted more. More space. More light. More room for Reya to run and grow. More roots to lie down.

The search began. We visited models by Drees Homes, Lennar, LGI—each one promising possibility. Raleigh caught our eye. The schools were a big factor, maybe too big. We feel that education is like armor when raising a Black daughter in a world where curiosity isn't always seen as brilliance, and presence is often mistaken for defiance. Durham was home. It held our memories, our roots. Raleigh held our future. At least, that's what it felt like.

Chris never wanted to sell. He loved our first home. But we needed that equity to step into the next one. So, we did what we had to do. When I found the perfect house on the perfect lot, everything moved fast. Faster than I expected. Maybe that's how blessings show up—rushing in right before your knees buckle.

Reya was two now. Walking, talking, throwing tantrums, asking questions like "Why is it hot?" and "Where is Daddy?"— her voice full of wonder, her heart still untouched by shame. She was curious and wild and tender and loud. I was trying to balance being a wife, a mother, a Realtor®—and now, her hairstylist.

When Deja, Chris's older sister, moved in, something shifted in our home—and in me. She had just come down from Charlotte to change careers and join the automotive world, but what she really joined was our village. Without asking, without fanfare, she became a steady hand and a soft place to land.

Tall and graceful, with warm brown skin and long, honey-brown locs that framed her face like a crown, Deja carried herself with a quiet confidence that was hard to ignore. She had effortless beauty—makeup or not; you looked twice. It was her energy that made you stay. She had sharp cheekbones, kind eyes, and a laid-back style that somehow always felt put together. There was strength in her frame but softness in her presence, a mix of elegance and approachability that made people feel safe around her.

When it came to Reya's hair? She was magic. The kind passed down through hands that knew softness could still be strength. Deja could part, twist, and moisturize like she'd inherited the gift from the ancestors themselves. For a while, I let her lead with quiet gratitude, relieved to have someone so loving and patient in a space where I still felt like I was fumbling.

Deja's impact went beyond hair. She saw me. She saw Reya. She showed up—not just in our home, but in our lives. In the in-between moments. The ones you can't post, but you feel forever. Not just for photos, but for the messy middle. Fatigued nights. The toddler tears. The mornings when I needed help without asking. She became a sister, not by blood—but by choice. The woman who lifts others even when her own arms are full.

When she moved out, I realized how much of a presence she had become in our lives. While I was nervous to take the reins, I also knew her love had left a legacy. Every time I picked up the comb, I felt her spirit in the room whispering, "You've got this." But that negative self-talk always seemed to get the best of me.

I stood in the bathroom with Reya one Sunday, comb in one hand, coconut oil in the other. She looked up at me with skeptical eyes, the same eyes that used to scream, "Anyone but her." And for a moment, I froze. I could feel the old narrative creeping in: *You're not good at this. You're an athlete, not a mother with magic hands. Let someone else do it.*

It wasn't just about hair. It was about pride. It was about identity. Every time I ran a comb through her curls, I remembered the pain of being told—silently or directly—that my Blackness was too much. A white boy who broke up with me because loving me came at a cost. A woman in Poland who looked at me like I didn't belong. That shame used to sit on my scalp like a secret. I wasn't going to let Reya carry that. Not in her crown. Not in her skin.

Every braid was a small revolution. A silent promise: *You are not too much. You are a masterpiece.* Then, I remembered something my sister Sade once said: "Shanda, you can totally do this. It's not as hard as you think."

"Bullshit," I whispered to myself back then, defeated.

The competitor in me? She doesn't go down easily. So, I started small—two or three plats, a twist here, a part there. Reya cried less. I smiled more. And I kept going.

Those Sunday mornings became sacred. Me, Reya, and a tablet playing slime videos while I moisturized and braided, fumbling through YouTube tutorials and Pinterest boards like my mama was watching. Because in a way, she was. She'd spent thirty years behind the chair, and I was finally beginning to understand the legacy in her hands.

Motherhood isn't about knowing everything. It's about showing up—again and again, with love and intention, even when you feel you're winging it.

That year stretched me. Real estate was harder than I had imagined. Being a wife, mother, entrepreneur, and hair whisperer was no joke. But it also taught me something:

I was not just becoming the mother I thought I'd be. I was becoming the woman I was fated to be.

For a while, that truth felt like enough.

The noise quieted. My footing felt sure. Our roots deepened. Until they didn't.

Even when you've finally found your rhythm, life doesn't ask permission to change the beat.

SEEN WITHOUT EXPLANATION

*T*he day we closed on our new home in Raleigh, I cried more tears. Not because I was sad. But because no one told me how heavy dreams can feel when you're the one carrying them. When they stop being wishes and start being responsibilities.

It was everything we wanted — space, a yard, a better school district for Reya. New construction again. Our thing. Fresh walls and blank rooms that felt like a clean slate. We were building forward. Together. But beneath the celebration, I felt something fray. Not ungrateful—just quietly unraveling.

Chris's commute had tripled—eleven miles in Durham had turned into thirty-six. Reya's new academy was only 6.2 miles from the new house, but from Chris's job. Thirty-one. The math made it clear. I handled the drop-off. I handled the pickup. I was everything in between. While that made the most sense logistically, it didn't feel fair emotionally. Logic doesn't always soothe the soul—especially when the load falls unevenly.

I was proud of us. Proud of him. Chris had just received another promotion, achieving his highest position yet as Director of Sales. His career was flourishing. His leadership is held in high esteem. No one had a stronger work ethic than his. He left before the sun came up and didn't return until it was setting. He never complained. Never missed a beat. Yet, I'd be lying if I said there weren't days I silently asked, what about me?

I had gone back to work—not because Chris asked me to, but because I needed to remember who I was before nap schedules and dinner prep. Being needed wasn't the same as being seen. My ego demanded it. My sanity depended on it. The legacy I wanted for Reya required it. Trying to be everything at once was slowly breaking me in places no one could see.

I juggled showings and toddler tantrums, offers and overdue laundry, educational worksheets and emotionally drained clients. Real estate wasn't just a job—it was oxygen. It gave me permission to take up space again. To have my name on something that mattered. But every reclaimed piece came at a cost.

Dinner, for instance.

Cooking was something I hated. I still do. I was an athlete my whole life—people cooked for me. I never had to think about what was for dinner. Now, it was my daily responsibility. When I didn't cook, when we ordered takeout "again" or resorted to leftovers, I felt like I was failing—again. Not because Chris said anything. He never did. But his question on the way home — "What's for dinner?" A question so simple on the wrong day sounded like a verdict.

It wasn't just the food. It was the house. The 3,600 square feet of clutter and crumbs and clothes and chaos I tried to tame every day while balancing contracts and client calls. It was keeping Reya's hair moisturized, her behavior managed, and her imagination nurtured. It was being a wife, a mom, and a businesswoman— and somehow being excellent at all of it.

Chris would come home and greet me with love, "Hey, how was your day?" but all I had was a faint smile and the dry phrase, "It was good." He thought I was angry. Maybe I was. But mostly, I was exhausted.

We didn't communicate well back then. Not the way we do now. He didn't know what I was feeling because I didn't tell him. I waited for him to interpret my silence, forgetting that silence isn't a language most men understand. I expected him to see it, sense it, solve it—without ever saying a word. When he couldn't, I resented the silence. I wore my hurt like armor and mistook his peace for detachment. We weren't at war. We were just two tired people trying to love each other while drowning in the weight of unspoken things.

"I don't know what's wrong with you," he'd say, looking at me with that confused, loving face.

"I'm fine, nothing is wrong," I'd respond, folding laundry like I was putting away pieces of myself.

Then there were moments of grace. Like when a client hugged me and said, "Thank you, you really helped me through a dark time." Or when Reya said, "Mommy, I like your hair today," completely unaware that I'd cried the night before over not feeling beautiful or seen.

There were daycare payments that felt like mortgage payments, early learning center tours that gave me guilt, and calendar blocks that looked like they belonged to someone with five jobs. There were flashbacks—deep, echoing ones—to childhood moments where I didn't feel wanted, except for what I could do. Not who I was.

Yet, I chose this. All of it.

Despite the chaos, I believed in it. In us. In me. I believed it would get better if I could just keep holding on.

Part of what I was holding onto wasn't even from this season of life. Some of the weight was older, deeper. After I was spat on in that parking lot, something inside me calcified. I stopped trusting people—and spaces. In restaurants, I had to face the door, always. My back could never be to a room. I walked faster into the house as if danger might catch me in the dark. When I lived alone, it felt like every shadow had eyes. That's why I moved into Chris's apartment before the townhome was completed. I didn't feel safe—not in public, and not always in my skin.

So letting Chris lead me, trusting his protection, surrendering control—it wasn't just new. It was terrifying. I wanted to feel covered, but I didn't know how to unclench. I didn't know how to breathe with both eyes closed.

One night, Chris found me standing in the pantry, holding a box of pasta like it held the answer to everything.

"You okay?" He asked.

"I'm good." I responded.

"No, you're not." He said.

He was right. I wasn't.

That night, I finally told him. Not all of it. But enough. Enough for him to know I wasn't mad at him. I was drowning in myself.

That moment cracked something open. It didn't fix everything, but it shifted the air between us. Gave me room to exhale. Gave him room to see me—not just the wife or the mother or the woman with the license—but the little girl who still sometimes feels like she's trying to be enough.

I'm not always the woman I imagined I'd be. But I'm still becoming her. Every time I show up, even tired, even unfinished, I am seen—with no need to explain.

I thought I was finally catching my breath.

The house, the work, the routine—it was all settling. But peace for women like me never stays long.

Just when I felt like I could carry it all without breaking, life added more weight. The kind that doesn't ask for permission or pause. The kind that reminds you: no matter how strong you've become, there are still stories that can shake your core.

This time, it wasn't just mine to carry. It belonged to the woman who taught me how to survive in silence...

It started with a phone call.

WHAT SHE SURVIVED, I CARRY

*J*ust when I found a rhythm again—just when the noise of guilt quieted—the ground beneath me moved.

Two days after Reya's seventh birthday, it happened.

A call that, though quiet, stills everything within you. The kind that steals your breath before it even speaks. The kind that forces you to return to the version of yourself who doesn't get to fall apart.

Only hold it all—again.

Maybe that's where this part of the story really begins.

Not in the moment everything fell...

... But in the quiet truth I had been carrying long before. In the guilt, the grief, the grit I'd inherited before I even had words for them.

I was seventeen the first time the word cancer moved into our lives without permission.

It was January 2005—the year life around me felt like it was crumbling, before everything would finally line up for our family. Prior to Rashad, my brother, winning a national championship at UNC. Before: Three straight state titles preceded my name. Before I would be on my way to Chapel Hill.

This is where the pain began.

Sade and I were waiting for my mom to come back from the store so I could get to practice. It was a normal afternoon. Nothing loud. Nothing alarming. Just my sister and me at home, bags packed, ready to head to the gym.

Then the phone rang.

I answered it.

A nurse was on the line asking for my mom. I told her she wasn't home yet and asked if I could take a message. The woman paused.

Then she said something she wasn't supposed to say.

"Her chemotherapy appointment is scheduled for next week. Please have her call us back."

That's how I found out my mom had cancer—over the phone. From a stranger. By accident.

I didn't even know what to say. I looked at my sister, stunned, and we both just kind of froze. The silence between us felt heavier than the words themselves.

Cancer.

It sat in my throat like a secret and spun in my mind like a warning siren. I called my mom right away and asked her if it was true. She had just found out herself. I could hear it in her voice— this mix of disbelief and maternal resolve. Her goal was not to frighten us. She tried to sound strong. According to her, they'd caught it early. The doctors had a plan. That everything would be okay.

When you're seventeen and you've already lost your grand-mother to the same disease, you don't really hear the details. You hear danger. You hear death.

I nodded along and told her it would be okay. I even believed myself for a moment. A few days later, after sitting in classrooms like nothing had changed and lacing up my sneakers like every-thing was the same, I broke down.

I couldn't carry it.

It was the scariest moment of my life.

Still—I went to practice.

We were in the middle of what would become our only undefeated season, the first three-peat in program history. Every drill was sharp. Every minute on the court had meaning. But I was floating through it.

I ran suicide sprints with a lump in my throat.

I boxed out while silently picturing my mother in a hospital gown.

I called plays while mentally counting days—measuring time by fear.

I was there. But not really.

That's the thing about being a high-level athlete—no one's checking for the pain behind your performance. If you're moving, you're good. If you're locked in, you're strong. If you're getting buckets, you're fine.

I wasn't fine.

My mom was about to lose her hair. Her strength. Her sense of control. And all I could do was keep playing.

Later that day, she arrived home and relayed information we were already aware of; however, hearing it from her perspective shattered me anew. It wasn't a death sentence; she said. It didn't mean goodbye. She vowed to fight. And she did.

She battled surgeries, chemo, and fatigue. She came to my games when she had every right to rest. Her presence, both physically and spiritually, was a testament to her character.

When I felt like I couldn't keep going, I thought of her. Not the version hooked up to machines. The version who told me: "I'm not leaving this earth anytime soon. I'm fighting this for y'all." She meant it. Because she stayed—so did I. Those words stayed with me longer than the diagnosis.

It wasn't just about survival. It was about presence. About love that showed up, even tired. About strength that didn't need to announce itself—it just kept going.

* * *

HER FIGHT, MY FOUNDATION

My mother is 70 now. Still the strongest person I know.

Looking back, I realize that moment didn't just change what I feared—it changed what I saw. From then on, I wasn't just her daughter. I was her witness. A witness to her fight, her faith, her quiet kind of power. The kind that wrapped itself around me with no need to say a word. The kind that said, *"I'm not leaving. I'm still here."*

She was. She still is. But not without more trials and tribulations.

After breast cancer came the hip replacements. Then the degenerative arthritis. Then sleep apnea. Heart failure (HFpEF). An enlarged pituitary gland. A brain aneurysm. High blood pressure. Diverticulitis. A colostomy bag that was later reversed. Chronic spinal pain. And still—she made it. Over and over again.

On December 17, 2025, the call came again.

She had failed a stress test.

The doctor didn't waste words. He said it the way mechanics talk about broken engines—direct, detached, decisive.

"She needs triple bypass surgery immediately."

There had been signs—shortness of breath, a tiredness in her voice — she brushed it off the way so many Black women do, quietly. With a deep breath. With a prayer that no one else could hear. With a strength that makes pain seem peaceful. Manageable until it becomes life-threatening.

I hung up the phone and stood still.

Not again.

Not her.

Please—God, not again. Not the woman who taught me how to be strong without showing the strain.

We were told she had been walking around with what's known as a widowmaker—a heart attack in progress that should've taken her.

Three arteries blocked.

The doctor presented three options: a stent, watch-and-observe, or full bypass.

There was only one choice. We were lucky to have it.

Chris was still at work. The company had just announced his promotion to General Sales Manager—his greatest accomplishment. I didn't know yet, but his face changed when I told him about my mom. He said little—he rarely does in a crisis—but he held me a little longer that night, swallowing all the pride he felt from his own personal achievement. We were both processing what this meant, not just for her—but for me, for us, for everyone who depends on the woman I had always known as invincible.

Braylen, my nephew, was already staying with us. My sister was deep in her own mental health struggle. She couldn't be present. And Aiyana, her daughter, stayed close to her side—which made sense. I was doing the same for mine.

That left us with a new, terrifying responsibility. Our family grew overnight.

Chris. Me. Reya. Braylen.

My father was as steady as ever, but even he looked tired. Rashad flew in from L.A. to be there. Thank God he did. The moment he walked into that hospital room, her eyes lit up. It was the first genuine smile we'd seen in days. She softened—exhaled. As if she had been holding her breath waiting for her babies to be in one place again.

We arrived at 4:00 a.m. for the surgery. When they wheeled her away, she whispered, "I love you, baby." "I know, Mama," I said. But inside, I was unraveling. Because once again, I was her anchor.

She survived.

Triple bypass.

A new scar. Another storm. Another silent miracle.

She came home on December 27th. The best late Christmas gift we could've ever received. Just when we breathed again, January arrived. January 16th, to be exact—my niece Aiyana's 19th birthday.

My dad called. "Something's wrong with your mom." "Call

her and tell me what you see." I FaceTime'd her immediately. She smiled. But something was off.

Her face was slightly drooping.

Her speech is sluggish.

Her energy dimmed.

I knew. Before the doctors did. Before the scan confirmed it.

A stroke.

One month after the bypass. For the first time in all her battles, I saw her scared. Not defeated. Not broken. Shaken.

I realized: The woman who had survived everything was human after all. At night, I would sit on the couch, blanket wrapped around me, scrolling through my thoughts like unpaid bills.

Braylen.
Reya.
Chris.
Clients.
Deadlines.
Worries.

My mother. It's always my mother. What she survived—I carry. Not just in memory. Not in duty. But in blood. In legacy. In the space between daughter and woman.

Sometimes when I look in the mirror, I see her looking back. Not just in face or form—but in fight. This chapter isn't just about illness. It's about the weight of survival. It's about the daughters who become caregivers, and the caregivers who still have to mother through it all. It centers on women—like Brenda—who never asked to be anyone's superhero...

But became one anyway.

THE GIRL WHO LIVED

I used to think healing looked like a perfectly sealed scar —neat, invisible, erased. Now I know it looks like a journal page that tried to kill me, and a life that refused to let go.

In March of 2002, I wrote a letter I never meant for anyone to read. Not because it was private—though it was—but because I didn't expect to still be here. I didn't think I'd live long enough to look back on that version of myself with anything but shame.

I was 15.

Smart. Athletic. Popular by default. Completely invisible in the places that mattered. No one knew I was unraveling on the inside. That the darkness in my chest was louder than my voice. That I was walking hallways with a full schedule and an empty spirit.

Then, one more thread came loose.

I had my first boyfriend that year. He was white. Kind. Bold. We weren't in love, but I liked him. He saw me. Or at least he tried.

After people saw us together, the whispers started. Then the slurs. And then, one day—it ended. He told me we couldn't be together. That people were calling him a "nigger lover," and he couldn't take it.

He was ashamed of me. Not for who I was—but for how the

world saw me. That moment shattered something I didn't know could break.

It wasn't just the breakup. It was confirmation.

My love always came with conditions. Even when I was chosen, it could be revoked. That no matter how smart, athletic, or "good" I tried to be—I would still be too Black to be worth standing beside.

So, I wrote this:

Dear you,
March 2002

I have continued to abuse myself and the people around me. I feel that I am a big mistake and just a problem to the world. I feel like the only way to make my life and the lives around me happier would be for me to be dead and out of their lives. All I have done is cause trouble and harm to myself and my loved ones. The question is what can I do about it. The answer is nothing. I can do nothing but die to make my life easier and stop the pain that I am causing to the people around. Today I took 9 pills. Last night I took 12. Each pill had 200 mg worth of drugs in it. Why did I do that—who knows, and really, who cares? No one cares. This morning, I woke up and I was still here. I was still alive and breathing. But why—I didn't understand. I just don't get it. Do I really have friends or is it just an act—an act to get close to me just so that you can hurt me again? I just don't get how this world works.

That wasn't a letter.

It was a scream.

A plea from a girl who felt she had nowhere to hide, no one to tell the truth to, no safe place to lay it all down. Back then, I didn't want to die. I just didn't know how to live like that anymore. That's when my father shifted. When the damage finally became visible.

That was the moment he said it.

"I love you."

I had never heard of it before. Not from him. Not from my memories. I didn't know what hurt more — hearing it for the first time or realizing how long I had been waiting for it.

He didn't understand that his way of loving me had made me feel like I had to earn breath. That silence shaped me as much as words ever could. But the truth is—my pain didn't begin at fifteen. That was just when it overflowed.

* * *

THE ACHE BENEATH IT ALL

I was young. Too young to understand what was happening, but old enough to feel it wasn't right.

A child in a church van headed to Bible study—no parents in sight, just neighborhood kids dropped off to be filled with God. We were told we were safe there. That the people inside those walls were good. Unfortunately, in the cold basement of that building, something happened that changed how I saw the world forever.

There's a silence that comes after certain kinds of harm. Not the kind you choose—but the kind that's forced on you. The kind that shows up in your body before your brain can make sense of it.

I didn't have the words for it then. What I had were instincts:

Don't speak.

Don't move.

Don't cry.

Make it go away.

But it didn't go away.

It lived in my shoulders, in the way I flinched when people got too close. In the way I overachieved, over-smiled, over-functioned. In the way I disappeared inside my skin and called it survival.

I didn't tell anyone—not at first. Not because I didn't want to. I didn't think it would change anything. I didn't want to ruin anyone's life. Silence felt safer than disbelief.

That silence shaped me.

It taught me how to read a room before I entered it. How to keep secrets in my body like they were mine to carry. How to build walls so high, even the people who loved me couldn't reach the girl inside.

It's taken me years to understand that what happened wasn't my fault. I was never broken—only guarded. That my strength didn't come from what I survived.

It came from what I *refused* to let define me.

I'm still healing. Still naming things I once tucked away in the corners of my mind like they didn't matter.

They do. Because what we don't name, we carry. I'm tired of carrying what never belonged to me.

This is not the entire story.

But it's the part I'm ready to tell.

* * *

REGRETFULLY, later in my life, it would happen again. And again. Not the assault, but the feelings that came with it.

Different rooms. Different faces. Different places. The same emptiness. The same emotion. The same shame, though not mine, still clung to me.

These were not random incidents. They formed a pattern. A blueprint of betrayal stitched across the years, each one reinforcing the same brutal message:

You are not safe here.

You are not seen here.

You are not sacred here.

I was tired of being the strong one. Tired of being the silent one. Tired of being unprotected.

So, I wrote a letter.

And I woke up.

Still breathing.

Still here.

Now, I look back on her—on me—with something bigger than pity. I look at her with reverence.

She survived.

She kept going.

She found breath again.

If I could, I would hold her face in my hands and say:

You are not a problem.
You are not too much.
You are not shame.
You are not what they could not say or see.
You are not the silence that raised you.

While some truths never made headlines... while justice came quietly, without apology or fanfare... I now understand:

Healing doesn't always look like winning.

Sometimes, it looks like telling your story without needing permission. Sometimes, it looks like *surviving long enough to speak for yourself.*

That is what I am doing now.

LETTER TO CHRIS

*D*ear Chris,
 There are so many things I wish I had the words to say sooner. Not because you asked for them, but because I carried them silently for so long—like invisible bricks on my back. Your love: your love for me has been profound in ways I haven't always understood. You remained by my side during my uncertainty. You supported me when I doubted myself. And you believed in me— even when I was unraveling.

You were never just the man I married. You were the mirror I didn't know I needed—the steady one, the anchor, the silent warrior who rose early and came home late, always trying to make sure we were good. Most days, we were. But I wasn't. I didn't know how to tell you that.

When I said, *"I'm good,"* what I really meant was, *"I'm drowning, and I don't know how to ask for help without feeling like I've failed you, or me, or both."*

I was never mad at you for working hard. I admired it. Still do. But some days, the distance between your 36-mile commute and my 6-mile loop of drop-offs, real estate calls, toddler tantrums, and guilt felt like a canyon. I resented the silence—not because of anything you did, but because I didn't know how to be honest about the noise inside me.

You never judged me. Not when I ordered takeout again. Not when the house wasn't perfect. Not when I cried over things I couldn't name. You just asked, *"What's for dinner?"* and I heard a challenge when it was really just a question. That's on me. My guilt, my pressure, my perfectionism. You didn't create it—but you helped carry it, even when I made it heavy.

You have given me safety. And stability. And space to become.

You've reminded me that I don't have to do everything to be everything. That love isn't measured by performance. That being tired doesn't mean I'm failing—it just means I'm human.

You are the father I prayed for and the husband I didn't know I deserved. The world doesn't always see you the way I do—your quiet strength, your goofy charm, the way you make Reya laugh when I'm too tense to find joy. But I see you. And I always have.

You married a woman who had walls. Who hid behind smiles. Who loved hard but trusted slow. Despite that, you stayed.

You told me once, *"Let's make it work. Just don't hide from me again."*

That sentence changed everything.

So, I won't.

This letter is my heart unhidden. It's not perfect, but it's honest. Like us.

Thank you for being the man who saw me. The man who stayed. The man who reminded me that having it all means nothing if you can't share it with someone who sees the mess and still chooses the masterpiece.

Love always,
Rashanda

LETTER TO REYA

*M*y sweet Reya,
   If you're reading this one day—maybe as a young woman, maybe as a mother yourself—I hope you know something I didn't always know: You were never just my child. You were the miracle that remade me.

You came after a storm I wasn't sure I'd survive. A loss that broke me. A silence that nearly swallowed me whole. And then, one April morning, I found out I was pregnant again—with you. From that moment on, I knew God had answered a prayer I couldn't even speak out loud.

You made me believe in light again.

Raising you hasn't always been easy, but it has always been worth it. The early days of sleepless nights, balancing real estate deals and daycare pickups, doing your hair even when I was exhausted—it all taught me how to show up for you in ways no one ever showed up for me. And I want you to know I didn't always get it right, but I never stopped trying.

I hope I've given you more than just structure and safety. I hope I've given you the truth. Permission to feel. The courage to ask for help. And the strength to stand tall in a world that sometimes tries to shrink strong girls into silence.

I see myself in you—your fire, your imagination, your heart that's too big for your little body. I want you to protect that. Even when the world tells you to dim your light, don't. Shine anyway.

You don't have to be perfect to be powerful.

You don't have to be strong all the time to be worthy.

You don't have to earn rest or love or peace. They belong to you.

I deeply pray that you will grow up knowing how deeply loved you are—not for what you do, but for who you are. If ever you forget, come back to this letter. Read it slowly. Let it remind you that your mother lived a whole life before you—but nothing truly began until you arrived.

You are my why.

My witness.

My legacy in motion.

So, if I ever leave this earth before I say everything you need to hear, let this be the loudest echo: I love you. I am proud of you. And you are never alone.

Love always,
~Mommy

EPILOGUE

WHEN HAVING IT ALL STILL HURTS—AND HEALS

I used to think healing meant the pain would stop. That if I got it all right—marriage, motherhood, the house, the title—the ache would finally let go.

It didn't.

The truth is, pain doesn't vanish just because your blessings multiply. It reshapes. It hides in quiet moments—school pickup lines, late-night laundry, perfectly folded lives that still feel like they're coming undone.

This isn't a book about regret. It's about reality. About what it means to live inside a life you built with your whole heart—and still question if you're allowed to feel overwhelmed. About being deeply loved, and still feeling invisible sometimes. About surviving things no one clapped for.

I wrote this not as a guide—but as evidence. That you can be whole and still healing. That you can have everything you asked for and still feel the weight of what it took to get here. That strong women still need soft places to land.

If nothing else, I hope this book gave you language for the ache. Not to dwell in it—but to name it. To move through it with grace. And to stop apologizing for carrying it.

Because the most sacred truth I've found is this: You don't have to be unbreakable to be worthy. You just have to be honest. And still here.

That is enough.

ACKNOWLEDGMENTS

To Chris and Reya,
You are the heartbeat behind every word on these pages. Chris —thank you for your patience, your strength, your belief in me when I struggled to believe in myself. Reya—my light, my why. You made me a mother, and in doing so, you made me more whole. I love you both beyond words.

To my parents, Brenda and James,
The yin to each other's yang. Your love has always been the soil beneath my roots. Thank you for being here to witness Reya grow, for staying alive through storms you didn't deserve, and for showing me what quiet endurance looks like. I'm better because you never gave up.

To my brother, Rashad,
You've always been my twin flame in this life. Thank you for never giving up on your dreams—and for pushing me to jump in the rain, even when I wanted to stay dry. Your courage has been my compass since childhood.

To my sister, Sade,
I pray this book meets you in a meaningful place. May it whisper to your own greatness and remind you of your voice— because it's powerful. Keep rising.

To Aiyana, Braylen, and Aria,

Even in moments of distance, you are a part of my lungs—pieces I need to breathe. I love you more than you know. Always.

To Ma and Pops—Sheila and Chris,

Thank you for raising a man who is respectful, hard-working, and gentle. Thank you for loving me as I am, for embracing my flaws, and for showing up with the kind of love that feels like home.

To Deja and Alexis,

You're my sisters in spirit, not just in name. Thank you for loving me so well. I'm not easy to read, but you never let me disappear into myself. You pull me out, call me higher, and love me anyway.

To Kassidi and Kairo,

I love you both deeply. Thank you for loving me back, in your own beautiful way.

To Cameron and Renee,

Thank you for loving me with a tenderness that transcends titles. You have stepped in like a mother and a brother when life asked more of my parents than they had to give. You've never asked for anything in return—you simply showed up. I will never forget that. I love you both endlessly.

To my mother's siblings—Sandra, Gail, Michelle, Renee, Uncle Brian (Tiger)

What an extraordinary legacy you carry. After losing your mother —my grandmother Mary—so young, you each became reflections of her strength, her softness, her fire. I never got to hear her laugh, but I see her in you. Thank you for loving me without conditions, for being my compass, and for reminding me where I come from.

To my cousins—Jasmine, Cameron, Camille, Destinee,

Brian, Justin, Trenton, Laila, Maxwell, Ava, Artis, and Canon

Life would never be the same without you in it. We've grown up, side by side, creating a joy so rich it still echoes in our adult hearts. You are my people. My peace. And my proof that family—when rooted in love—never fades.

To my father's sisters— Katherine and Angela,

As a little girl, I felt safe with you. I felt seen. I didn't always have the words, but I never had to ask for your love—it was just there. Thank you for that. Your spirits have left a permanent warmth in mine.

To my cousins—Shaconda, Joquish, Angelica, Keno, Dontarious, Kira, and Bri'aja, and Bri

Thank you for loving me even through distance. Life has taken us in many directions, but whenever we reunite, we don't miss a beat. That's love. And I'm grateful for it.

To the rest of my family

If your name isn't here, please know your place in my life still matters deeply. Your love and support helped build this book, whether through a call, a smile, or a quiet prayer. I'm thankful for each of you.

To Coach Sonita Warren Dixon,

You were the coach who saw past my game and into my heart. You showed up when I was unraveling and held space for me like no one else could. You listened. You taught. You loved. I became my best self on the court—and off—because of you. Thank you forever.

To my teammates

From Asheville High to UNC to the WNBA, from Israel to Finland, Sweden, and Poland—thank you. You were there for so many chapters—some painful, most beautiful. You taught me about grit, grace, and the power of team. I carry you all with me.

In Loving Memory

To my angels—those I can no longer hold but will always carry in my heart.

My grandmothers, **Mary** and **Edna**, whose quiet strength still echoes in mine.

My great-great-grandmother **Ellen (Mamma)**, whose legacy lives through every prayer I whisper.

Miss Maybin, whose presence was more than a name—she was a light.

My grandfather **William (Pete)**, who walked with quiet wisdom.

My cousins—**Marchae (25)** and **Gregory (15)**—losing you changed my world in ways I'm still finding words for.

Sheryl and **Dennis**, your love and laughter live on in my memory.

There are others I hold close in spirit, whose names may not all be listed but whose presence surrounds me still.

Thank you for protecting me, for guiding me, and for reminding me that I am never alone.

I love you forever.

ABOUT THE AUTHOR

Rashanda McCants Johnson is a former professional basketball player, WNBA draft pick, and University of North Carolina standout whose legacy stretches from championship courts to heartfelt conversations about identity, motherhood, and healing. A three-time ACC Champion, All-American Honorable Mention, and the first woman from UNC to appear on the cover of *Sports Illustrated*, Rashanda's story defies the highlight reel.

After stepping away from the game to support her family through illness and transition, Rashanda reinvented herself as a devoted real estate professional, wife, and mother—anchoring her success not in applause, but in purpose. Her professional journey reflects a fierce commitment to resilience, advocacy for truth, and creating generational change through both action and example.

She wrote *When Having It All Still Hurts* after a cancer scare forced her to confront what she had long been avoiding: herself. It began with a mammogram she nearly skipped and ended with a mirror she could no longer ignore. This book became her way of choosing herself, of documenting the unspoken emotional toll women carry, and of leaving behind more than stories—she wrote it to leave her daughter a legacy of truth.

Today, Rashanda uses her voice to uplift women navigating the quiet ache beneath success, and to remind them that wholeness doesn't require perfection—just the courage to be seen.